150 words
Starter

曹冲称象

Cao Chong Weighed an Elephant

许晓华 改编 李佳星 翻译

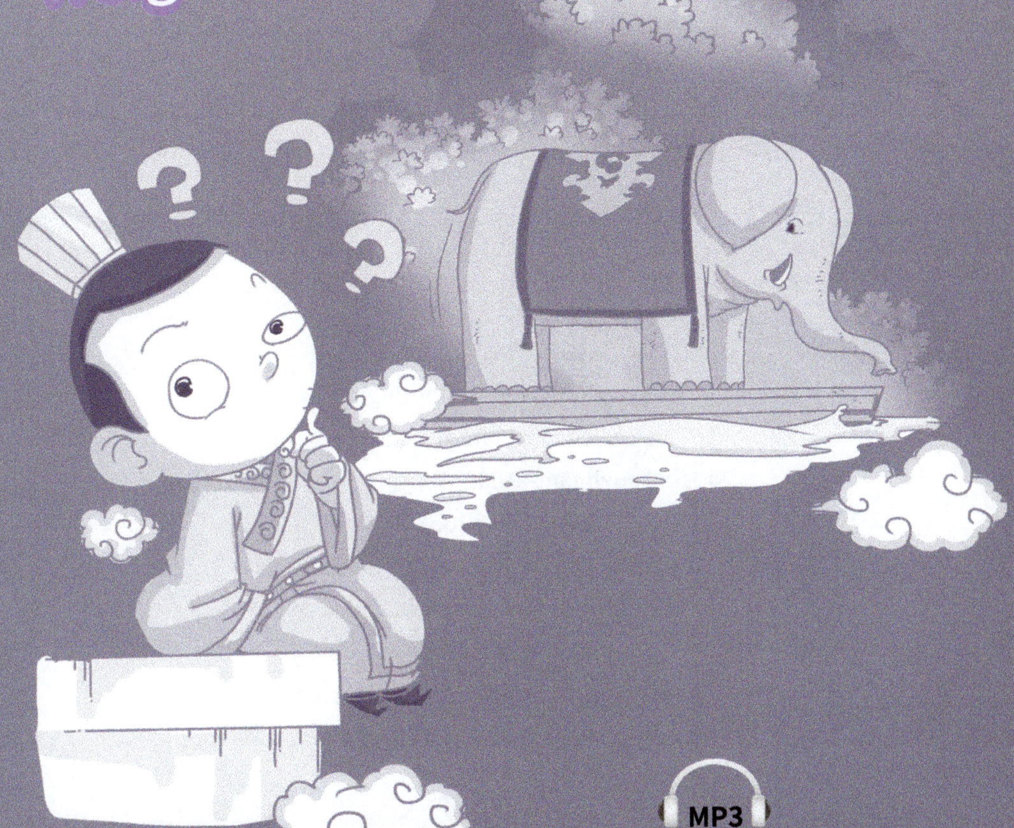

MP3
Download Online

SinolinguA
华语教学出版社

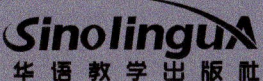

First Edition 2016
Third Printing 2018

ISBN 978-7-5138-1018-0
Copyright 2016 by Sinolingua Co., Ltd
Published by Sinolingua Co., Ltd
24 Baiwanzhuang Road, Beijing 100037, China
Tel: (86) 10-68320585 68997826
Fax: (86) 10-68997826 68326333
http://www.sinolingua.com.cn
E-mail: hyjx@sinolingua.com.cn
Facebook: www.facebook.com/sinolingua
Printed by Beijing Jinghua Hucais Printing Co., Ltd.

Printed in the People's Republic of China

编者的话

对于广大汉语学习者来说,要想快速提高汉语水平,扩大阅读量是很有必要的。"彩虹桥"汉语分级读物为汉语学习者提供了一系列有趣、有用的汉语阅读材料。本系列读物按照词汇量进行分级,力求用限定的词汇讲述精彩的故事。本套读物主要有以下特点:

一、**分级精准,循序渐进**。我们参考"新汉语水平考试(HSK)词汇表"(2012年修订版)、《汉语国际教育用音节汉字词汇等级划分(国家标准)》和《常用汉语1500高频词语表》等词汇分级标准,结合《欧洲语言教学与评估框架性共同标准》(CEFR),设计了一套适合汉语学习者的"彩虹桥"词汇分级标准。本系列读物分为7个级别(入门级*、1级、2级、3级、4级、5级、6级),供不同水平的汉语学习者选择,每个级别故事的生词数量不超过本级别对应词汇量的20%。随着级别的升高,故事的篇幅逐渐加长。本系列读物与HSK、CEFR的对应级别,各级词汇量以及每本书的字数详见下表。

---

* 入门级(Starter)在封底用S标识。

级别	入门级	1级	2级	3级	4级	5级	6级
对应级别	HSK1 CEFR A1	HSK1-2 CEFR A1-A2	HSK2-3 CEFR A2-B1	HSK3 CEFR A2-B1	HSK3-4 CEFR B1	HSK4 CEFR B1-B2	HSK5 CEFR B2-C1
词汇量	150	300	500	750	1 000	1 500	2 500
字数	1 000	2 500	5 000	7 500	10 000	15 000	25 000

二、**故事精彩，题材多样**。本套读物选材的标准就是"精彩"，所选的故事要么曲折离奇，要么感人至深，对读者构成奇妙的吸引力。选题广泛取材于中国的神话传说、民间故事、文学名著、名人传记和历史故事等，让汉语学习者在阅读中潜移默化地了解中国的文化和历史。

三、**结构合理，实用性强**。"彩虹桥"系列读物的每一本书中，除了中文故事正文之外，都配有主要人物的中英文介绍、生词英文注释及例句、故事正文的英文翻译、练习题和生词表，方便读者阅读和理解故事内容，提升汉语阅读能力。练习题主要采用客观题，题型多样，难度适中，并附有参考答案，既可供汉语教师在课堂上教学使用，又可供汉语学习者进行自我水平检测。

如果您对本系列读物有什么想法，比如推荐精彩故事、提出改进意见等，请发邮件到 liuxiaolin@sinolingua.com.cn，与我们交流探讨。也可以关注我们的微信公众号CHQRainbowBridge，随时与我们交流互动。同时，微信公众号会不定期发布有关"彩虹桥"的出版信息，以及汉语阅读、中国文化小知识等。

韩　颖　刘小琳

Preface

For students who study Chinese as a foreign language, it's crucial for them to enlarge the scope of their reading to improve their comprehension skills. The "Rainbow Bridge" Graded Chinese Reader series is designed to provide a collection of interesting and useful Chinese reading materials. This series grades each volume by its vocabulary level and brings the learners into every scene through vivid storytelling. The series has the following features:

I. A gradual approach by grading the volumes based on vocabulary levels. We have consulted the New HSK Vocabulary (2012 Revised Edition), the *Graded Chinese Syllables, Characters and Words for the Application of Teaching Chinese to the Speakers of Other Languages (National Standard)* and the 1,500 Commonly Used High Frequency Chinese Vocabulary, along with the Common European Framework of Reference for Languages (CEFR) to design the "Rainbow Bridge" vocabulary grading standard. The series is divided into seven levels (Starter*, Level 1, Level 2, Level 3, Level 4, Level 5 and Level 6) for students at different stages in their Chinese education to choose from. For each level, new words are no more than 20% of the vocabulary amount as specified in the corresponding HSK and CEFR levels.

---

* Represented by "S" on the back cover.

As the levels progress, the passage length will in turn increase. The following table indicates the corresponding "Rainbow Bridge" level, HSK and CEFR levels, the vocabulary amount, and number of characters.

Level	Starter	1	2	3	4	5	6
HSK/ CEFR Level	HSK1 CEFR A1	HSK1-2 CEFR A1-A2	HSK2-3 CEFR A2-B1	HSK3 CEFR A2-B1	HSK3-4 CEFR B1	HSK4 CEFR B1-B2	HSK5 CEFR B2-C1
Vocabulary	150	300	500	750	1,000	1,500	2,500
Characters	1,000	2,500	5,000	7,500	10,000	15,000	25,000

II. Intriguing stories on various themes. The series features engaging stories known for their twists and turns as well as deeply touching plots. The readers will find it a joyful experience to read the stories. The topics are selected from Chinese mythology, legends, folklore, literary classics, biographies of renowned people and historical tales. Such wide-ranging topics exert an invisible, yet formative, influence on readers' understanding of Chinese culture and history.

III. Reasonably structured and easy to use. For each volume of the "Rainbow Bridge" series, apart from a Chinese story, we also provide an introduction to the main characters in Chinese and English, new words with English explanations and sample sentences, and an English translation of the story, followed by comprehension exercises and a vocabulary list to help users read and understand the story and improve their Chinese reading skills. The exercises are mainly presented as objective questions that take on various forms with moderate difficulty. Moreover, keys to the exercises are also provided. The series can be used by teachers in class or by students for self-study.

If you have any questions, comments or suggestions about the series, please email us at liuxiaolin@sinolingua.com.cn. You can also exchange ideas with us via our WeChat account: CHQRainbowBridge. This account will provide updates on the series along with Chinese reading materials and cultural tips.

Han Ying and Liu Xiaolin

主要人物
Main Characters

曹　操（Cáo Cāo）：中国古代的一个大官，是一个很有才华的人。

Cao Cao: A talented person who used to be a key official in ancient China.

曹　冲（Cáo Chōng）：曹操的儿子，是一个很聪明的孩子。

Cao Chong: A son of Cao Cao and a child prodigy.

中文故事

曹冲称①象②

① 称 (chēng) *v.* weigh
e.g., 这些水果有几斤？你称一称。

② 象 (xiàng) *n.* elephant
e.g., 这只大象正在吃东西。

③ 汉朝 (Hàncháo) *n.* the Han Dynasty (206 BC – 220 AD)

④ 大官 (dà guān) *n.* senior official
e.g., 他的爷爷以前是一个大官。

一千多年前，中国汉朝③有一个大官④叫曹操。

曹操是一个很有才华①的人，他的权力②也很大。很多事皇帝③都要听他的。

① 才华 (cáihuá) *n.* talent
e.g., 他很有才华，工作做得很好。

② 权力 (quánlì) *n.* power
e.g., 老板的权力很大，你别跟他对着干。

③ 皇帝 (huángdì) *n.* emperor
e.g., 李世民是中国唐朝一位很有名的皇帝。

① 年纪 (niánjì) n.
age
e.g., 你今年多大年纪了。

② 聪明 (cōngmíng)
adj. smart, intelligent
e.g., 我的哥哥很聪明。

曹操有个儿子叫曹冲。曹冲年纪①很小，却很聪明②，曹操很喜欢他。

有一次，有人送给曹操一只大象，曹操很高兴。他带①了很多人去看，曹冲也去了。

① 带 (dài) v.
bring, take
e.g., 我带你去我家。

① 腿 (tuǐ) *n.* leg
e.g., 姐姐的腿很长。

② 粗 (cū) *adj.* thick
e.g., 他的腿很粗。

③ 耳朵 (ěrduo)
n. ear
e.g., 小猫的耳朵很灵敏。

④ 鼻子 (bízi) *n.* nose
e.g., 他的鼻子很大。

这只大象又高又大，腿①粗②粗的，耳朵③大大的，鼻子④长长的。曹操带的人，都没有见过大象。今天看见大象，大家都很高兴。

他们一个一个地走过去,有的摸①摸它的腿,有的摸摸它的鼻子。

① 摸 (mō) v. touch, feel
e.g., 你摸摸,这是什么?

还有的人走过去,和大象比一比,大象比他们高多了。

这时候，有一个人说："这只大象一定很重①！"曹操也说："这只大象真大！它有多重呢？你们谁有办法②知道？"

① 重 (zhòng)
adj. heavy
e.g., 他的书很重。

② 办法 (bànfǎ) n.
solution, idea
e.g., 我有一个好办法。

① 说话 (shuō huà) v. talk, speak
e.g., 他看着我,不说话。

② 一会儿 (yíhuìr) n. a while
e.g., 我过一会儿再打电话给你。

但是,没有一个人说话①。大家都在想办法。过了一会儿②,有一个人说:"我有一个办法。"

曹操问："你有什么办法？"那个人说："要知道大象有多重，可以找一个秤①来，一称就知道了。"

① 秤 (chèng) n. steelyard, scales
e.g., 我有一个秤，可以称东西。

大家说："可是，这只大象太大了，我们的秤都不能用。""那，我们就做一个大秤。"那个人说。大家都说，这太难了！这个办法不好。

这时候,曹冲坐在旁边,想着什么,什么也没有说。

① 切 (qiē) *v.*
chop, cut
e.g., 妈妈做饭，我切菜。

② 块 (kuài) *m.w.*
piece, lump
e.g., 我吃了一块糖。

又有一个人说："我看，我们可以把它杀了，切①成小块②，一小块一小块地称。"

听他说完,大家都笑了。大家说:"这个办法也不好。这只大象多好啊①!杀了,太可惜②了!"曹操也说:"这只大象不能杀。"

① 啊 (a) *exclam.* (used to express admiration or surprise) ah, oh
e.g., 天气多好啊!

② 可惜 (kěxī) *adv.* regrettably
e.g., 那个地方很好,可惜,我没有时间去。

① 别的 (biéde)
pron. other
e.g., 这个地方不好，我们去别的地方，好吗？

大家想了很多办法，但是曹操觉得，每个办法都不太好。他问："谁还有别的①办法？"没有人说话了。

这时候,他听到一个人说:"爸爸,我有个好办法,可以知道大象有多重。"曹操一看,是他的儿子曹冲。

曹操笑着说："大家都没有办法，你这个小孩子，有什么好办法？你说说，我听听，你的办法好不好。"

曹冲走过来,小声地把他的办法说了。曹操听了以后,笑了,他觉得儿子的这个办法很好。他说:"我们就用这个办法!走,我们去河①边。"

① 河 (hé) *n.* river
e.g., 河里有很多鱼。

① 条 (tiáo) *m.w.* (for sth. long, narrow or thin)
e.g., 一条鱼 / 船 / 河

② 船 (chuán) *n.* boat
e.g., 我们坐船去上海。

大家都想知道,曹冲有什么好办法。他们跟曹操一起到了河边。河里有一条①大船②。曹冲叫人把大象拉到了船上。

大象为什么上船?大家都不明白①。他们在河边看着,谁也不说话。大象上船了,因为它很重,船身②就一点点地往③下走。

① 明白 (míngbai)
v. understand
e.g., 我不明白,他为什么不想来。

② 身 (shēn) *n.* body, main part of a structure
e.g., 船身 / 车身

③ 往 (wǎng)
prep. toward
e.g., 他在上边,你往上看。

① 线 (xiàn) *n.* line
e.g., 一条线

过了一会儿,船身不往下走了,曹冲在船身上画了一条白线①。白线和水面一样高。画完白线,曹冲就叫人把大象拉下船。

他叫人拿来很多石头①，有大的，有小的。人们把这些石头拿到船上，船身又一点点地往下走。

① 石头 (shítou)
n. stone
e.g., 这块石头很重。

等船身上的那条白线和水面一样高了,曹冲说:"好了,不要拿了。你们称一称这些石头吧。石头有多重,大象就有多重。"

这时候,大家都明白了,说:"这真是个好办法!这个孩子真聪明!"曹操也很高兴。他看着儿子,想:"我的儿子真聪明啊!"

English Version

Cao Chong Weighed an Elephant

Over one thousand years ago, the Han Dynasty ruled over China. Cao Cao was a key official serving the Han Dynasty.

Cao Cao was a talented and powerful man. Even the emperor had to follow his ideas on many issues.

Cao Chong was one of Cao Cao's sons. He proved to be a smart child at a young age and was favored by his father.

On one occasion, an elephant was sent as a gift to Cao Cao, which made him very happy. He brought many people to see it and Cao Chong was among them.

The elephant was very tall and massive, with thick legs, big ears and a long nose. People were delighted to see an elephant for the first time.

They went closer to it one by one. Some touched the elephant's legs while others touched its nose.

Some went to compare their height with that of the elephant and the elephant was much taller than them.

At this moment, someone said, "This elephant must be very heavy!" Cao Cao agreed, "It is a big elephant! I want to know what it weighs. Can anyone figure out how to weigh it?"

No one answered him as they were all thinking of a way. After a while, one spoke up, "I've got an idea."

Cao Cao asked, "What's your solution?" The man said, "We can use a steelyard to weigh it."

People said, "This elephant is so large that none of our steelyard will work." "Then we can make a bigger one," the man answered. People thought it was too difficult to make one and it was not a good idea.

Cao Chong was sitting aside in deep thought, and didn't say anything.

Then another man said, "We can kill the elephant, cut it into small pieces, and then weigh each piece."

Everyone laughed at the absurdity of his idea and said, "It's not a good idea either. It's a wonderful animal and such a pity to kill it." Cao Cao also said, "We can't kill it."

People proposed many solutions but Cao Cao didn't find a single good one. He asked, "Do anyone have other solutions?" No one answered him.

Right at this moment, Cao Cao heard a voice, "Dad, I have a good idea to weigh the elephant." Cao Cao noticed that it was his young son Cao Chong.

Cao Cao said with a smile, "None of the adults here can work out a good idea. Do you, my little boy, really have a good idea? Tell us now."

Cao Chong whispered to his father his solution. After hearing it, Cao Cao smiled and knew it was a good idea. He said, "We will do it his way. Let's go to the riverbank."

People wondered what Cao Chong's idea was and followed them to the riverbank. Then Cao Chong asked someone to bring the elephant to a big boat in the river.

People didn't know what was going on and looked on without saying a word. The elephant stepped into the boat and the boat started to sink.

After a while, the boat stopped going down and Cao Chong marked the level of the water on the side of the boat with white paint. Once he was confident in the measurement, he asked someone to help the elephant disembark.

Then he asked people to put stones, big and small, into the boat and watched as the boat started to go down again.

He asked them to keep piling the stones on until the water reached the level he previously marked. Then he said, "Okay, stop putting more stones. Now weigh the stones. The weight of the elephant will be equal to that of the stones."

At that moment, everyone understood him and shouted, "Great idea! What a clever boy he is!" Seeing his little boy perform so well delighted his father so much!

课前练习 Warm-up exercises

一、朗读下面的短语。Read the following phrases.

tuǐ cūcū de　　qiēchéng xiǎo kuài　　biéde bànfǎ
腿粗粗的　　切成小块　　别的办法

yì tiáo dà chuán　　huàwán bái xiàn
一条大船　　画完白线

二、思考题。Pre-reading questions.

1. 想知道大象有多重，为什么很难？

2. 曹冲的办法是什么？

课后练习 Reading exercises

一、阅读故事，完成问题。
Read the story and answer the following questions.

1. 这个故事有两个主要人物，他们是 _____ 和曹冲。

2. 按照正确的顺序排列下面的句子。

   A. 曹操想知道大象有多重。

   B. 有人送大象。

   C. 曹冲想了一个好办法。

   D. 大家去看大象。

   E. 别的办法都不太好。

   （1）____ （2）____ （3）____ （4）____ （5）____

二、为下列各题选择正确的答案。Choose the correct answer according to the story.

1. 曹操是汉朝的（　　）。

   A. 皇帝　　B. 大官　　C. 国王　　D. 敌人

2. 曹冲是曹操的（　　）。

   A. 朋友　　B. 女儿　　C. 弟弟　　D. 儿子

3. 用"秤"可以知道东西有（　　）。

　　A. 多重　　　B. 多高　　　C. 多大　　　D. 多长

4. 在这个故事里，大家一共想出了（　　）办法。

　　A. 一个　　　B. 两个　　　C. 三个　　　D. 四个

5. 船上的石头和大象，哪个重？（　　）

　　A. 石头　　　B. 大象　　　C. 一样重　　D. 不知道

三、判断题：请根据故事内容判断下列说法是否正确，如果正确请标"T"，不正确请标"F"。
Decide whether the following statements are true (T) or false (F).

1. 曹冲想知道大象多重，所以大家想办法。　　（　　）
2. 用第二个人的办法，大象会死。　　　　　　（　　）
3. 白线跟水面一样高。　　　　　　　　　　　（　　）
4. 船上的石头都很大。　　　　　　　　　　　（　　）
5. 大家都觉得曹冲很聪明。　　　　　　　　　（　　）

四、看图复述故事内容。Fill in the blanks to retell the story using the pictures.

1. 曹操是一个很有才华的人,他的权力_____。很多事皇帝都要_____。

2. 这只大象_____,腿_____,耳朵_____,鼻子_____。

3. 曹操说:"这只大象真大!它_____?你们谁_____?"

4. 有一个人说:"我们可以_____,切成小块,_____地称。"

5. 河里有_____。曹冲叫人_____。

课后练习答案 Keys to the exercises

一、阅读故事，完成问题
　　1. 曹操
　　2.（1）B　　（2）D　　（3）A　　（4）E　　（5）C

二、为下列各题选择正确的答案
　　1. B　　2. D　　3. A　　4. C　　5. C

三、判断题：请根据故事内容判断下列说法是否正确，如果正确请标"T"，不正确请标"F"
　　1. F　　2. T　　3. T　　4. F　　5. T

四、看图复述故事内容
　　1. 也很大　听他的
　　2. 又高又大　粗粗的　大大的　长长的
　　3. 有多重　有办法知道
　　4. 把它杀了　一小块一小块
　　5. 一条大船　把大象拉到了船上

词汇表
Vocabulary List

啊	ex-clam.	a	(used to express admiration or surprise) ah, oh
办法	n.	bànfǎ	solution, idea
鼻子	n.	bízi	nose
别的	pron.	biéde	other
才华	n.	cáihuá	talent
称	v.	chēng	weigh
秤	n.	chèng	steelyard, scales
船	n.	chuán	boat
聪明	adj.	cōngmíng	smart, intelligent
粗	adj.	cū	thick
大官	n.	dà guān	senior official
带	v.	dài	bring, take
耳朵	n.	ěrduo	ear
汉朝	n.	Hàncháo	the Han Dynasty (206 BC – 220 AD)
河	n.	hé	river
皇帝	n.	huángdì	emperor
可惜	adv.	kěxī	regrettably
块	m.w.	kuài	piece, lump
明白	v.	míngbai	understand
摸	v.	mō	touch, feel
年纪	n.	niánjì	age
切	v.	qiē	chop, cut
权力	n.	quánlì	power
身	n.	shēn	body, main part of a structure
石头	n.	shítou	stone
说话	v.	shuō huà	talk, speak
条	m.w.	tiáo	(for sth. long, narrow or thin)
腿	n.	tuǐ	leg
往	prep.	wǎng	toward
线	n.	xiàn	line
象	n.	xiàng	elephant
一会儿	n.	yíhuìr	a while
重	adj.	zhòng	heavy

项目策划：韩　颖　刘小琳
责任编辑：韩　颖　彭　博
英文翻译：李佳星
英文编辑：张　乐
英文审订：黄长奇
设计指导：战文庭　卞　淳
设计制作：isles studio

图书在版编目（CIP）数据

曹冲称象：汉、英 / 许晓华改编．— 北京：华语教学出版社，2016
（"彩虹桥"汉语分级读物．入门级：150词）
ISBN 978-7-5138-1018-0

Ⅰ．①曹… Ⅱ．①许… Ⅲ．①汉语－对外汉语教学－语言读物 Ⅳ．① H195.5

中国版本图书馆CIP数据核字（2015）第230158号

曹冲称象

许晓华　改编
*
©华语教学出版社有限责任公司
华语教学出版社有限责任公司出版
（中国北京百万庄大街24号　邮政编码 100037）
电话：(86)10-68320585　68997826
传真：(86)10-68997826　68326333
网址：www.sinolingua.com.cn
电子信箱：hyjx@sinolingua.com.cn
新浪微博地址：http://weibo.com/sinolinguavip
北京京华虎彩印刷有限公司印刷
2016年（32开）第1版
2018年第1版第3次印刷
（汉英）
ISBN 978-7-5138-1018-0
定价：15.00元